Thank you for the
Support

09/04/20

FINDING
MY WAY

TITI POWERS

BALBOA.PRESS
A DIVISION OF HAY HOUSE

Balboa Press books may be ordered through booksellers or by contacting:

Balboa Press
A Division of Hay House
1663 Liberty Drive
Bloomington, IN 47403
www.balboapress.com
1 (877) 407-4847

Because of the dynamic nature of the Internet, any web addresses or links contained in this book may have changed since publication and may no longer be valid. The views expressed in this work are solely those of the author and do not necessarily reflect the views of the publisher, and the publisher hereby disclaims any responsibility for them.

The author of this book does not dispense medical advice or prescribe the use of any technique as a form of treatment for physical, emotional, or medical problems without the advice of a physician, either directly or indirectly. The intent of the author is only to offer information of a general nature to help you in your quest for emotional and spiritual well-being. In the event you use any of the information in this book for yourself, which is your constitutional right, the author and the publisher assume no responsibility for your actions.

Any people depicted in stock imagery provided by Getty Images are models, and such images are being used for illustrative purposes only.
Certain stock imagery © Getty Images.

Print information available on the last page.

ISBN: 978-1-9822-4945-8 (sc)
ISBN: 978-1-9822-4944-1 (hc)
ISBN: 978-1-9822-4951-9 (e)

Library of Congress Control Number: 2020910506

Balboa Press rev. date: 06/05/2020

CONTENTS

ACKNOWLEDGEMENTS

I want to acknowledge a few people that have helped me along the way on this journey to writing my first book. First, I want to thank God for watching over through everything I have been through. It hasn't been easy dealing with some of the darkest aspects in my life. The struggle didn't just start yesterday or the day before. It has been a continuous struggle from the time I was born because the way I was born was a struggle itself. Without the great mercies of God, I would not even be able to share my story right now. God has been good to me in so many different ways and I am thankful for everything He has done for me. He continues to do wonders for me in so many ways I can't take for granted.

I want to thank my son; He may still be too young to understand the impact he has had on my life. Some days when I felt like giving up, he was the one constant that stayed with me and helped me get through the tough days. Some days I was reminded that I am only doing whatever I am doing for him to have a better future. He is a big part of my life and I want to be able to provide him the best way I can. This is all for him and his future. He has given me so much courage to walk through life with confidence that things always get better at the end of the day.

I want to thank my good friend Morgan. She has been a huge blessing

since I met her. Her and I met in an unconventional way and she accepted me without any judgement. She has helped me with so many aspects in my life that I can't stop talking about. There are so many things to say about her that I discuss in the book. She believed in me more than any other person I know. She is not only my friend, but she is also the person that helped me write this book. When I met her, she mentioned that she was a writer. I asked her to write my book for me, which she agreed to do without any questions. She is a very big part of this book because she listened to all the details and wrote everything as I envisioned it. This book would probably not be written right now if it wasn't for her believing in me and my story. I am thankful for the support and encouragement she gives me every day to accomplish everything I set my mind to. She has truly been a blessing from God and become family to me.

I also want to thank my young sister. She was the only person that never gave up on me even when I was going through some dark days. She always checked on me even when my family was against it. She never once turned her back on me. She never forgets me regardless of where she is. We can be in different states, but we still find time for each other when we can. She understands me and I understand her.

I want to thank my husband for the love and support he has given me since he came into my life. He has added positive energy to my life and has so many plans for our future.

Last but not least, I want to thank all the new people in my life that I am meeting along the way. They might not know much about me yet, but the beauty of life is meeting new people and making sure they know who I am and vice versa. There are so many relationships that didn't work out for me, especially all the bad friends. However, I am starting to meet some new people in my life that finally believe in everything I do. Life is a little easy when you have people around you who support your dreams and encourage you every day.

INTRODUCTION

I have been thinking about writing a book for a very long time because of the struggles I have experienced in my life. This book is very personal and represents the struggles I have experienced on this journey to find my way. I can't say everything has been bad in my life; Like most people, I have had both good times and bad.

I witnessed how my parents struggled from a young age, and part of it followed me throughout all my life. I got the opportunity to come to America and thought life would be better, but I still faced some struggles from the time I got here

When the opportunity to write a book came, I couldn't pass on it because I know my story is a very unique one. I am not a victim, and I believe sharing the struggles I have experienced will help others. My story shows how far I have come and where I am going. I have seen both the good and bad side of life. My hope is that this book will assist people who are going through the same things I have encountered in life and encourage them not to give up so easily. I was just a little girl born in one of the smallest and poorest countries in West Africa. I never thought I would write a book, but I want to be able to share my story with some people that have gone through the same struggles as me. This is just my journey to finding my way. I will not stop until I accomplish that.

CHAPTER 1

EARLY LIFE

I was born in a small district in the Eastern Province of Sierra Leone, West Africa. It is a small town where most people know and depend on each other for a lot of different things. I have a difficult time remembering everything I experienced when I was a child because it is too painful, but some of the bad things are just hard to forget.

My siblings and I did a lot of the same things many children do. We had play dates; we went to some of the best schools. I was social and outspoken and had many friends. I always had a positive attitude and loved to socialize. I enjoyed doing a lot of things, especially dancing. I loved being the life of the party and would go out of my way to entertain people around me.

There were also some rough times along the way. Families in the neighborhood were often violent toward each other. Therefore, at a very age, I was exposed to things I thought were normal but shouldn't have been. I grew up seeing old people – close and distant relatives fighting every day, and I thought that was okay and normal. People would fight one day and wake up the next day acting like nothing had happened

Growing up this way taught me to believe that it was normal to fight and then let it go like nothing ever happened in the first place.

The violence alone would have been bad enough to worry about, however during this time as a very young child me and my older sister Racheal faced a big challenge that every girl our age had to go through. In my culture, girls growing up are supposed to be circumcised.

Female genital mutilation is mostly common in West African countries. When it came to circumcision, I wouldn't say we were forced into it, but rather brainwashed. We had no idea what it entailed or why it had to be done. Martha, an old lady in my village, made that decision for us. She said we had to go through with it.

I only learned about female circumcision later in life due to cultural differences and education. It was one of the toughest things to go through especially at such a young age, but we endured the pain and because that was the expectation of every girl that age. This time made me miss my family who wasn't around me more because as a young girl going through that, the one comfort you need is from your family. My family wasn't around me because everyone had gone to different places. My parents were not together anymore, hence my mother moved to a different city. My siblings were in different parts of the country living with other relatives as we dealt with all the changes that were taking place in the home.

This particular decision not only affects you because of the pain you experience when it is done, but it also affects the relationships down the road. Most of my relationships were hard to keep because I didn't have the one thing men were looking for. Men in my culture or most cultures I have been around don't usually go for women that are circumcised. Hence, it made it hard for me to find a man that was okay with me telling them I was circumcised.

3

CHAPTER 2

LIFE DURING THE WAR

When I was about three years old, a war broke out in my hometown. My hometown had a lot of diamonds, therefore, different people used to come to the town trying to get a piece of the diamonds. Rebels later discovered people were coming to get the gold and were benefiting off it, and decided they wanted a piece of it too.

The rebels started killing innocent people because of the diamonds, and the town became very unsafe. People had to leave the area and flee to the city. We were one of the families that had to leave.

When we moved to the city, we had to start a new life and go to school. It was especially hard for me, as a young child, to move from a small town to a big city. I was the second born out of the four of us children, so I had to help my younger siblings even though I was still a young child myself.

Overall, life in the city was beautiful for a while. Our relatives gave us almost everything we wanted. They took us to the beach, and they made sure we got to experience everything a little child would like in the city. I loved being with my siblings and enjoying all the good things the city had to offer. We were happy kids because we were too young to

understand much of what went on around us. We supported and loved each other through both the good and bad times.

A couple of years later, the civil war broke out in the whole country. The war spread from our old town to the city where we now lived. Our parents calmed us down and told us they were going to get someone to take us to a neighboring country, Guinea, where we had relatives.

My parents gave Racheal and the guy that was taking us to our relatives some money to help us with the whole process of moving. The guy picked us up and took us to a station where other people who were fleeing the country were getting on large trucks.

Every day, the trucks were loaded with hundreds of people. The conditions on the trucks were miserable: there was no breathing room, nowhere to turn, and no space at all. But we had to endure it because that was the only way to get out of the country.

The truck drivers warned everyone to keep quiet because they did not want the rebels to know anyone was on the trucks. Even though our legs ached from standing so long and we had bruises from bumping up against people, we had to keep calm and not make a sound.

After what felt like an eternity, the trucks stopped. The driver came out and said he'd just gotten word that the rebels were in the next city we were supposed to pass through. The news scared us so much that it was even harder to stay quiet.

The drivers said they were out of money and could not bribe the rebels anymore. The only option was for us to get down and run through the bush for the remainder of the journey.

I still remember the horror on everyone's faces when the drivers delivered that news to us. Racheal wondered out loud what we were going to do. She had to take care of us because my parents had given her that responsibility. No one knew where we were. There was no way of communicating with our family because there were no cell phones.

Racheal helped me out of the truck, and we started looking for places to spend the night. So were all the other people who had been on the trucks with us. We began knocking on doors asking different people to let us in their homes for the night. It was pitch black and could not continue moving that same day. We finally got a room with six other people. We slept on the floor all night… it was freezing, but that's the best we could get.

The next morning, Racheal said we would follow everyone and go wherever they were going. She calmed us down and told us we would be fine, and God would lead us.

As we started moving on foot, all I could see were dead bodies everywhere, burned houses. The villages were destroyed—it looked like a tornado had passed through them overnight. It was horrifying for a kid to witness, but there was no time to stop and be comforted if we didn't want to be left behind.

There was someone always in the front of our group who would hurry ahead and scout the area to see if it was safe to keep going. If it wasn't, we'd have to move in a different direction. Sometimes we even had to backtrack if none of the directions we wanted to take were safe.

Throughout all this struggle, for days we had no food. We were hungry and tired but couldn't stop or the rebels would catch us, and we had to keep going until we found a safe place for the night. To keep from starving, we ate whatever we could find on the ground, sometimes even dust. It sounds like an exaggeration, but when you're that hungry any and everything looks good. It was a very trying time.

After two weeks of traveling on foot, we finally got to a city on the border of Freetown and Guinea, where everyone who escaped the war came to. We were dirty, exhausted, and starving, but the only one of those things we cared about was food. When you're moving to save your life, the last thing you think about is being tired.

We were lucky to meet a guy who knew our parents. He bought us food and drinks, and we were thrilled to have normal food after going so long without having a proper meal.

We didn't know how tired we were until we got to a safe place. You don't think about being tired when your life is in danger. Two weeks on foot is nothing when you have the fear of being killed in the back of your brain, especially when you're hearing gunshots and looking at dead bodies along the way.

It is amazing how God protects us without us even knowing. We were so thankful for the good Samaritans who offered us something to eat when we got to the safe place. Once we were rested and our bellies were full, it was time to think about our next steps.

CHAPTER 3

MOVING FROM FREETOWN TO GUINEA

Although it was rough along the way, having hope that we were going to make it to the next city and out of the war kept us going. I do not know if it was luck or God's grace, but when we got to the city, there were a few family members that were able to help us transition. After so many struggles, we were happy to see some people we knew. We moved into one of our Aunt's big homes, and they soon made us feel like we were part of their family. It was good to reconnect as we tried to forget all the bad times we went through. It was harder because I was so young but going through the war is something that will always be part of my story.

Now, due to the fact that there were so many people living in the same house, an unfortunate event happened to me when I was there. This is probably one of the hardest things for me to talk about because no kid should ever experience what I experienced. In fact, very few people know about it.

While I was living with those relatives, I was molested. A man called me into a room and said he wanted to send me to the shop to go get something for him. His room was so dark, and I was hesitant to go in

there. But he insisted and said I should go in there or he was going to beat me up.

I said no and tried to run outside, but he grabbed me from behind and began taking me to his room. I kept saying no, but he said he just wanted to give me the money. He was older than me by a lot—about twenty-five, and at that time I was only ten.

I kept saying no to him and that I could not go into the room with him because it was so dark in there. But he wouldn't listen and finally got me to the room.

Once we were there, he grabbed me from the back and put his fingers in my vagina. At this point, I did not know what to do. I was so scared and tried to scream. He put one of his hands over my mouth so that I couldn't. He played with my vagina for what felt like five straight minutes.

I kept begging him to stop, and he finally stopped. When I was walking out of the room, he told me not to tell anyone. He said that would be our secret—if I ever told anyone he would beat me.

Because of the fear he put in me, I couldn't tell anyone and didn't know what to do or how to handle what happened. I held on to that secret for a very long time and couldn't share it with anyone. I did not have anyone to tell because he came to me again and said if I told anyone, he would kill me. He started buying me different things every day to bribe me and keep me quiet. I struggled with the secret for a long time and didn't know how to live with it. A few months later, Racheal and I moved to Gambia to join my cousins there. I hoped living there would help me forget that bad experience and let me create new memories. I was so excited to move to a different country and start over.

We began a new life there and went to school for a while, trying to fit in as quickly as possible. We took care of each other and leaned on each other for protection. We thought life was going to be good, but it

took time to forget everything we had gone through prior to moving to Gambia.

We later finally moved back to Guinea for a few years, and finally moved back to our home country because the war was done. We moved in back with our relatives who we stayed with in Freetown during the war.

It was a wonderful being reunited with my siblings and close friends again. I was still very fragile because of everything I had experienced. I used to talk my way out of any confrontation.

The only person who wouldn't let me get away with anything was my younger brother Bob. I was always adventurous - I used to try different things like; climbing trees, playing with sharp objects, running in the middle of the road, playing dangerous games with people that were more mature than me, and eating in places I wasn't supposed to be eating. He didn't want me to do some of the things I was doing because he didn't want me to hurt myself in the process. That ended up causing fights between Bob and Racheal because she defended me every time he beat me up. Through a series of experiences Racheal and I became closer.

Freetown had so many good memories for me. Because I'm a free spirit, I made friends and had a lot of fun there. I also spent quality time with my siblings. I was used to the lifestyle in Freetown, and for sure thought it was going to be challenging to move back to Guinea.

At that time moving back to my relatives made a lot of sense, and it later opened an opportunity for me that very few people get to experience living in Africa. It might not have been an aspiration of mine, but no one would ever turn down a great opportunity especially if it is going to make life better in so many ways.

CHAPTER 4

COMING TO AMERICA

After living in Guinea for a few years, a great opportunity to come to America came up. I had just finished my high school exams and was wondering what my next plan would be. I had so many dreams and goals set for myself and was excited to see where life would take me. For example, I wanted to be a model because I had participated in a contest and won, I wanted to be a radio presenter because I am very articulate - just to mention a few dreams I had. And out of the blue, a great opportunity came my way.

I always thought I was going to live all my life in Africa. But my family had the opportunity to move to the U.S., and I was excited to experience living there. I dreamed of becoming a model, actress, or some kind of celebrity.

I moved to Minnesota and started a new life with most of my family members, my brother, sisters, and extended family. For the first few months, I was sad because I missed all my friends, my family, and my life back home in Freetown and Guinea. It took me longer than I expected to get used to the American lifestyle. I was bored and had

nothing to do. I had no one to talk to. I was definitely frustrated and wanted to go back to my home country.

However, I sat down and thought about my situation and decided to stay strong.

I had just finished high school in Guinea, but the education levels are way different. There are more-developed African countries with good education systems like the ones here in America. It was just unfortunate that I didn't get a chance to get that level of education before coming here.

I knew very little English, and I wanted to learn more. I missed having friends. Because of the differences in the educational system, I was eligible to enroll in high school, so that's what I did.

The first few months in school were difficult. I spoke very little English prior to coming to the U.S.A., so I had a hard time understanding most of the material, and that was frustrating. Eventually, I began to understand what was taught in school and that helped me stay focused. There were a lot of things I was taught in school here in America that I wasn't taught back in my high school in Guinea. Once I began speaking English more fluently, things became a lot easier for me.

My decision to go to school was the best thing I did for myself when I came to America. It was humbling to start over like someone who hasn't been to school at all. However, going back to gain basic knowledge and starting from zero helped me a lot along the way.

Starting over is never easy, but sometimes it is necessary. I wouldn't have been able to find myself without gaining that knowledge. That is why I say my life in America started when I went back to school. I not only got an education and learned how to speak and read English, but I made new friends. I didn't appreciate how important friendships were until I had to live in a new place with no friends. The new friends I made in school helped me feel a lot more comfortable here in America.

They helped me get through the hard days when I was really missing my friends and family back home. I finally fit in.

My friends made me feel at home. I always wanted the best for those around me and went out of my way to ensure everyone was happy. I was soon taught a few valuable lessons for being too trusting.

CHAPTER 5

MEETING MY FIRST LOVE

I'd been living in America for a year when I met a man I thought was the love of my life. We bonded from the first time we met and officially started going out a few months later. We had great energy, chemistry, and connection, and we couldn't stay away from each other.

When my family found out I was seeing him, most of them were not happy. They worried that I'd abandon my dreams. What they said didn't faze me because I was in love. Nothing they said would make me leave him.

He and I were happy together for over a year until I got pregnant. I was so young and dumb and didn't know much about contraceptives. No one had ever told me anything about protection, and I had never used any before. In fact, I didn't even know I was pregnant for about four months. I found out when I got sick.

My cousin and I had just gone to a party and I became so sick. We went to the hospital that same night to find out what was happening.

The doctor came into the room after running some tests and said, "Do you know you are four months pregnant?"

I was shocked. I told the doctor, "That is a joke and impossible.

There is no way I am pregnant." I was on my period and couldn't believe it.

The doctor confirmed the news—I was actually pregnant. I started crying because I didn't know what I was going to do and what I was going to tell my family.

My cousin asked, "What are you going to do?" That added to my anxiety and panic because my family still disapproved of the whole relationship. I knew I was in trouble. They weren't going to take the news lightly.

At that time, I was living with a lady named Morgan. After I left the doctor's office, I went to her home and told her about the news. I was so nervous because in my culture I was not allowed to have kids out of wedlock. I was crying because I had brought embarrassment to my own family. I was also crying because when I moved to America, my original plan didn't include a relationship and getting pregnant within the first year. I cried my eyes out.

Morgan listened to me cry, then sat me down and said, "This is life . . . things happen that you don't plan for. At this point, we cannot take anything back. We have to let your family members know about this pregnancy."

At first, I said no because I was scared of what my relatives would say. I later agreed to call and tell them because a pregnancy is not something that can be hidden forever.

The first person I called was my Aunt Rebecca, who I was close to. When I told her I was pregnant, she started screaming and yelling, "Whoa! she is pregnant!" Without saying anything else to me, she hung up and called everyone she knew.

Before I told anyone else about the pregnancy, I told Morgan that I didn't want to keep it. I was scared because I didn't know what the rest of my family back home would do when they found out.

I told Peter that I wanted to abort the pregnancy. He was disappointed because he was excited and wanted to keep the baby. I told him I had to take it out because if my family back home found out I was pregnant; it was not going to be fun for anybody—especially him because he impregnated me without me knowing about contraception. He begged me to keep it, but I said no.

I later decided to go to the hospital to have an abortion… I took the abortive pill and waited in the waiting area. When it was time for me to go into the exam room, they told me that I had to get an ultrasound first.

During the ultrasound the nurse informed me that, "Unfortunately we can't take out the pregnancy because you are beyond four months pregnant. The only way you can take it out is by going to a specialist."

I said, "That is a joke; this is not happening . . ."

She assured me that it wasn't a joke. I could not believe it. She told me how risky it was to have an abortion after that many months into the pregnancy. But I was willing to take the risk., so the nurse gave me the number for the specialist.

I called the specialist while still in the office only to find out she was traveling for vacation and would be back in a month. A month from then would be far too late.

I went home and told Morgan that we needed to figure out another way to end the pregnancy. She told me to go to bed and that we would figure it out later.

She prayed into the morning hours before she got some sleep, and the next morning she told me she had a dream and that I should keep the baby. She said if I ended the pregnancy something bad would happen (she was a very prayerful woman). She said the child would grow up to be a blessing to me even if I didn't feel or think it was at the time. Mind you, while Morgan was telling me all this, Peter's family

was calling me to tell me to keep the baby. He had even gone to his church and asked the pastor and everyone to tell me to keep the baby.

After listening to what everyone had to say, and after a lot of reflection, I decided to keep the baby. I also decided to call my relatives to tell them about the pregnancy.

Matilda my stepmother back home was very upset and started yelling over the phone as soon as she found out I was pregnant, "How could you do this to me after all the pain we went through to help you get to America!"

I could feel her pain and didn't know what to tell her. I struggled to find the words. "I understand, but I wasn't planning to get pregnant when I moved here."

She was so upset and said she would never talk to me again, which I understood because in my culture we are taught at an early age not to get pregnant until we are married. Even though I knew she would have that reaction, it was hard to take in at first. But as a young pregnant woman, that type of abandonment is hard to take especially if it's something you didn't plan. I didn't think their reaction was going to be that extreme.

I was so lost for a few months living with my family and didn't know what to do, but I decided to move in with Peter and figure things out from there. I figured moving in with him would make more sense because that would give us the opportunity to get through the pregnancy and raise the child together.

My family came to see me and asked me to go home with them and go back to school.

I declined their offer and told them I wanted to stay with Peter because I loved him and wanted to be with him. Upon hearing that news, they told me if that is what I wanted to do, they were never going to talk to me again and didn't want anything to do with me.

I said okay and stayed with my boyfriend, and that is pretty much where all my new struggles with moving in with Peter and coming to America started.

I struggled through the rest of my pregnancy, crying every day and asking God to take the pregnancy. I could not understand why my family would abandon me because I was pregnant. I was devastated and depressed because I didn't have a job, and I didn't know what to do because I was so young.

I was in the hospital almost every day because of anxiety symptoms. Some of them were not even pregnancy related, but I had to go to the hospital because of anxiety pretty much.

I didn't have anyone to lean on because Peter was the only one working. We were frustrated because money was tight. We were living in a low-income housing apartment and pretty much had nothing. Some people will say I should be happy I had a roof over my head. I would say those people are right thinking that way. However, being pregnant and not knowing what the future holds is one of the scariest things in life.

It would have been okay if it had just been me and my boyfriend living that way. But I was scared every time I thought about my unborn child coming into this world and having to suffer. It wasn't their fault or choice to be born in that type of environment. There was very little I could do except pray and hope things would change. I didn't know how long we were going to live in that particular situation with very little help, and that contributed to my depression.

CHAPTER 6

HAVING MY SON

One night, Peter came back from work, and I woke up with sharp stomach pain. I was very uncomfortable; I could not sleep, sit, or stand because I was in a lot of pain. I was only eight months and half pregnant, and the baby wasn't supposed to be born yet.

Our next-door-neighbor and friend Jamal helped Peter take me to the hospital. Jamal's Aunt was right behind us on the way to the hospital. We got there at two a.m., and I gave birth to a baby boy at eight a.m.—a quick, easy birth without an epidural or any medicine to help me.

Jamal's Aunt asked us if we had car seat or clothes for the baby. We didn't. We weren't expecting the baby to come early, so we had nothing for him to wear. I hadn't even had time to bring clothes for myself to change into.

She went and bought us baby clothes and a car seat. I was very thankful and grateful because I didn't know how we were going to get any of those things.

Then she asked us if we had a name for the baby. We didn't. All the nurses kept asking us if we had a name for him. Since we hadn't chosen

one yet, they temporarily called the baby his dad's last name for a few days until we came up with a name for him.

After three days in the hospital, Peter came up with the name "Shaka." I

"Shaka?" I asked him.

"Yeah." He then explained that he'd grown up in Botswana, where a movie called *Shaka Zulu* was made. Shaka Zulu was a great warrior who was born to a family who never really wanted him, but he later grew up to become a great warrior. Peter said because of all the struggle I went through, Shaka would be a great name.

I agreed with Peter after listening to the story and his reasoning. We named our child Shaka and left the hospital a day later.

I was excited to go home because I thought Shaka would bring some happiness to our lives. It ended up being the absolute opposite. As soon as we went home, Peter and I started having fights every day and night.

I had no one else who lived close by to turn to. The only person from my family who would talk to me was my young sister Jen who loved me and checked on me every day by calling me. She had to be very careful though because if they caught her, she would get in trouble.

I was very depressed and sad, yet I had a child to take care of. We did not have any food at the house; we had to go to the food shelf to get food to survive. Even when we had food, I could barely eat because I was sick and sad all the time. Though we had some good times during our relationship, most of my memories from that time are of fights between me and him.

When Shaka was two years old, Peter and I made a conscious decision to stop fighting and instead, try to create a family. We got married. I wanted our son to grow up in a happy family because I did not have one growing up. All my childhood memories were of

people fighting, and I did not want my son to grow up in that type of environment.

Looking back to the time before we were married, I knew marriage to Peter was probably a bad idea because we fought all the time, but I thought that if I left him, I was going to be unhappy and no one would want to be with me. That was a very bad way of thinking because I ended up marrying him for the wrong reasons— he was not good for me or my son. But I was very insecure and had no one to turn to for help, so I convinced myself I was doing it mostly for Shaka. I thought that was the best way to get Peter to settle down and be in our lives.

After the wedding, though, we still fought. The police were at our house almost every night. Once I even spent a night in jail because Peter called the police on me, and they ended up locking me up for the night.

Through all this, I still went back to him after every fight. I did not want my family to laugh at me or tell me, "We warned you about that guy; he is not good for you." Because of that, I decided to stick it out for a while.

Even though I was living in a toxic relationship, I managed to finish high school and later met a nice woman named Nancy who mentored me. She helped me rediscover myself because she gave me different advice from daycare help, to what I should do with my life. Things definitely got a little better when I met her because she helped me get back on my feet and gave me the courage to go through all the adversity. I decided to move on with my life because I was not going to sit around and wait for my family to forgive me. I realized I was just hurting myself thinking they would one day come around. I told myself I had my own life and had to start living it by doing things that made me happy. I realized that if I didn't move on, I was only hurting myself and not them.

It took me a while to realize that because I loved my family and hoped they would change their minds. They didn't.

When I finished high school, I went to college, but it was rocky because I had to be in and out of college. Sometimes we had no food or no babysitter. It was hard for me to attend classes and stay in school.

A few months later, I started talking to my siblings. I even remember one day my uncle Marcus came to visit and said hi to all my siblings but not me. I was devastated and sad because that made think no one wanted me and my son.

I decided to keep my distance from my family because most of my family members had yet let go of the anger they had towards me. I had a few friends, but they were not very helpful. They didn't motivate me or help me when I was doing something wrong. I loved making people happy, and I sacrificed just to please other people. My friends figured that out and used me any time they could. I did not see it, or I just ignored it because I needed friends since no one in my family was talking to me at that time because I had left them. I later figured out they were not good friends and decided to seek a better life for me and my son.

I eventually decided to separate from Peter because nothing was working. I tried to stay for various reasons: I was scared that no one else was going to ever want me; I was going to be miserable alone with just me and my son; I didn't want my family to tell me they told me so, and because I loved him. But I finally realized that it's never a good idea to stay with someone for the wrong reasons—you will just end up hurting yourself. The only way I could have stayed in that relationship is if I fully believed he would change.

Why did he need to change? Well, Peter cheated on me with multiple women. He disrespected me so much, but I stayed because I thought I could change him. We were never happy. We moved house to house,

living in people's basements on the floor without any furniture. I spent my time taking care of Shaka, and Peter refused to work hard to get us out of that miserable situation.

I asked myself if that was really the life I came to America for. I was broken and destroyed and had to do something about that, especially for my son. One day, I packed all my things, put everything in the storage, took Shaka, and walked away.

I lived with my friend and cousin for a few months praying and crying every day. Even after moving out though, I still thought I would eventually get back with Peter. I prayed every day and begged him to come back to me and work on the relationship because I wasn't yet fully ready to let him go. It was a painful situation because he didn't care and had already moved on, but I was still begging him to let me come back. I finally pulled myself together and decided to move on with my life.

CHAPTER 7

MOVING TO NEW YORK

Eventually, I decided I needed a fresh start and moved to New York, where I met a nice, older guy named Jay. He said he saw a lot of potential in me. I was susceptible to that because I was very fragile and needed some guidance.

The first thing he told me to do was to cut my hair off. I was like, "Cut my hair off? You must be crazy!"

He explained what he meant. He wanted me to start a new life. He showed me a lot of things, like what it meant to be loved by someone deeply. He treated me well; he loved me and my son. He took care of me and Shaka the two years we were together. I didn't have to work even once the whole time.

Jay treated me like a real queen. When we went out, people thought I was some type of celebrity because I was so well dressed. He wanted to marry me and even proposed one year into our relationship. I said yes to the proposal. We had a great time together, but not everything was always roses and gold. We had normal issues that all other relationships usually have. We traveled to different places, and he gave me so many

things I needed and wanted, but all those couldn't make up what I was still missing in a man.

On top of our relationship issues, my relatives refused to accept him because he was a musician and well-known back home. Everyone thought dating a musician was a bad idea. He was even willing to convert to Islam just to impress my family, but that wasn't enough to change anyone's opinion about him.

At that time, I was starting to get back on good terms with my family. So, the fact that my family didn't fully accept him weighed on me a little bit too. I didn't want to rock the boat. I didn't want to go back to being on their bad side, and I had to make a choice that would benefit me and my son.

We ultimately decided that the relationship just wasn't working, and I moved back to Minnesota. Although we broke up, he is still one of my great friends. We still call each other sometimes and have nice, long talks. Sometimes I call him asking for advice because he was the first person who told me my future was going to be bright because he saw a lot of potential in me. I will never forget him regardless of where I live or whom I meet. He will forever be that friend I can count on.

In addition to all the above reasons I had for leaving Jay, I wasn't fully over Peter. We weren't divorced when I'd moved on with Jay; I believe that also played on my mind and made life a little bit harder for me. New York is beautiful and many people dream of living there, but it isn't the right place for everyone. I learned it wasn't the right place for me.

CHAPTER 8

GOING BACK TO MINNESOTA

When I moved back to Minnesota Jay and I broke up, I decided to give Peter a second chance. I thought after two years we would be able to get back together and things would be different. I thought the time apart would heal all wounds, but I was wrong. The second time was way than worse the first time . . . we were fighting more than we were before.

By that point, Shaka was 5 years old and going to school. He saw us fighting every day before he went to school and after he got home. It was a toxic environment because every time we fought; we would break everything in the house. I can't blame all the fights on Jay; I had my anger issues too. When someone pissed me off, I went from zero to a hundred really quick.

Peter brought up so much anger in me because he disrespected me. We didn't trust each other. He didn't show appreciation for anything I did for him even after all I went through to be with him. He refused to give me a proper wedding that my family could be part of. I told him that having a wedding celebration would help bring my family back into my life, but he wouldn't do that for me.

I stayed in that relationship for another four more years before I was so tired that I filed for divorce. Even with all the problems we had, he couldn't believe it when he got the divorce papers.

While I was with Peter, I kept moving from job to job because I had no support for my son. I had to leave these jobs to take care of my son because I was the only one there to take care of him. One of the best jobs I had was as flight attendant. Jay had originally introduced the idea to me because he thought I would be great at it.

I went to travel school to get my flight attendant degree. I enjoyed that job a lot because it was one of my passions when I came to America. Among the many dreams I had, my other dreams were to either become a model, or chef, or flight attendant. Being a flight attendant was everything I had hoped it would be. There was way more perks than I had ever anticipated. I traveled to places I couldn't have imagined going to. The best part was that my family was able to travel with me to some of the best places.

Being a flight attendant isn't always easy, especially when you have to leave your family for a few days at a time. Leaving Shaka behind for some of the trips was incredibly hard. He was still a little baby then, but I had to do what was best for the both of us since I was the sole provider.

On top of struggling with leaving Shaka and finding childcare for him, living with Peter meant that we were again moving from house to house. Back when I was just starting that job, Peter offered to find us a place to stay because he knew someone in Phoenix where I was stationed. He introduced me to some lady that he called a friend. He said me and my son could live with her until I found my own place. I was so happy that he had found us a place to stay while we got on our feet.

We lived with the lady until we later moved out. A few years later, I found out that the lady was actually Peter's ex-girlfriend. He was

very smart not to tell me that he was going to make us stay with his ex-girlfriend because he knew that I would never agree to such a thing.

We eventually found another place to live, but that didn't mean the struggles stopped. I made good money as a flight attendant but was unable to save any. We still needed extra income for the three of us to have a good life. The situation became very frustrating and started weighing heavily on me. With the lack of help raising my son and lack of financial help, the burden grew bigger and took a toll on me. I stayed with the job as long as I could because I was doing something I loved. However, every time I had to go home after my trip, I wasn't happy because of all the struggles I had outside the job.

I ultimately had to sacrifice my dream job for both my and Shaka's well-being. I didn't want to quit, but I had to because I wasn't getting any support from my ex at all. It wasn't even so much of the financial help that I needed from him. I just needed him to take care of our son, but he wasn't able to do that simple task.

From then on I focused on my family. We were still moving often because we couldn't afford a place of our own. We depended on people to take us in for however long they could in the hopes that we would get on our feet.

In the end, I left about six different great jobs because my husband couldn't be there to support me or my son. All I wanted was to figure my life out because I wanted to create a better life for my son.

As I was going through the divorce and trying to rediscover myself, I got a new job. I prayed every day and asked God to lead me to a nice, kind person who would understand me. Somebody who would change me and help me with my anger issues.

As life would have it, I met a great friend Morgan at my new job. I immediately felt that I could trust her, and that she would be there for me. I felt connected to her right of way, but she initially said she could

never have a friend like me because I talked too much! Later though, we became great friends, well, more like sisters. Next to Shaka, she was the best person who ever came into my life—like an angel sent from God.

One day, when I was so broken and hurt, I called her and asked if I could trust her. I told her my whole life story in what felt like one breath, and she listened. That blew my mind because all I have always wanted is someone to just listen to me and understand me.

She listened without saying anything. When I was done, she comforted me, took care of me, and guided me.

She was about to go Africa for vacation, but she said that she would be there for me any day and through everything. Any time someone tells me it's their birthday I try to go out of my way to do something for them. She said she wanted an Apple watch and I got it for her for her birthday. She was so surprised and happy… she couldn't believe it that I got her the Apple watch. She was in Africa for about a month, but I made it a point to call her every day and connect with her.

She's still my closest friend. She takes all my crap and doesn't judge me or make me feel like I can't do anything. Since I met her, everything changed. I started seeing life differently. My anger issues got better because of what she taught me. Anything I want to do; she encourages me and tells me that I can do it. Sometimes I feel like she knows me more than I know myself. She's brought so much joy and happiness in my life and made me think about life differently. Sometimes I look at her and ask her if she's an angel.

My friend sat me down and said "you know what… you need to focus on you and your son, a great man would come…" She was right.

Later, in a joking way, I told her that I should try online dating again. She set up a profile for me and said she'd talk to guys on my behalf, but if things got serious, she would give me the profile to take over. Through her intervention, I met a nice guy and we started talking. It's been good so far…

CHAPTER 9

RESTAURANT IDEA

I have always had a passion for starting my own business but just wasn't sure what exactly I wanted to do. I have a lot of business ideas, but I am yet to start one because of timing, financial reasons, and recently I didn't have the support I needed to commit to any business venture.

Most of my business ideas disappear because I either don't have anyone to discuss them with, or I don't have the necessary support system needed to start one. Now that my life is starting to settle down a little bit, I have started thinking about my business ideas again.

One night when I was sitting home stressed from my job, Morgan and I started discussing potential jobs or things that interest me. She suggested I follow my passion. She asked me what exactly I think I would enjoy doing. Without any hesitation, I mentioned cooking. and the idea of starting a restaurant.

My friend looked at me and said: "let's do it…" She told me if that is really my passion, she would support me.

I met a guy at my job and talked to him about it. He told me about a program that helps new entrepreneurs. He connected me with them,

and I signed up. I finished the class and now have a business proposal. The next step is to look for locations and money to start up the business. I know God is on my side. I put the idea on hold for a time until I figure out my new life and where I want to relocate to.

I've lived in Minnesota most of my life, but I have been thinking about moving to a new state to start over. I'm thinking it will likely be Atlanta, Georgia.

I'd eventually love to have one restaurant here in the U.S. and possibly one in Africa. At some point, I'd like to move back to Africa permanently because that's where I grew up, and I am familiar with all food-related things there. This whole process will not be easy, but with the new strong support system I have, I am very confident it will happen and work out for me. –It would be amazing to have a business doing something that's one of my greatest passions—cooking.

My friend even helped me come up with the idea of running a restaurant, since I love to cook. I got really excited about it and even made a plan. When I'm finally in a position to carry out my plan, I will be successful because of my friend and the strong support system I finally have around me.

CHAPTER 10

PRESENT LIFE

I have gone through a lot of struggles since I moved to the U.S. as a little girl. Most of the memories I have had until now have been bad ones. From not knowing who was really there for me, to a lot of people using me, to having a child at a such a young age with very little to no support, I have pretty much been on my own since I moved to this country.

I have worked so hard to get me and my son to this stage. Nothing has been easy for me and him, but I had to stay strong for both of us. I worked a couple of dream jobs but was never able to keep them because I didn't have a good support system for me and my son. I have traveled to so many places, but it's hard to even remember any good memories until recently.

I am still struggling because I haven't yet been able to keep anything good. I feel like one day I have it, the next day I don't have it. I am not as motivated as I was when I first came to the U.S. I had so many big dreams and wanted to accomplish every single one of them.

Lately I don't feel like I am motivated to do anything at all. I have my restaurant dream and I know in order for it to work, I have to put

in the work. I haven't been able to go to school again to better my life or even come up with more ideas for my restaurant. I know I have to keep fighting to get out of this funk, but it hasn't been easy. I continue to do odd jobs just so I can survive and continue to provide a stable home for me and my son. I have left countless jobs because none of them could accommodate my son's schedule.

Sometimes I wonder if it is just me thinking that things aren't working out, but I later remember how far I have come. It often feels like I am stuck in the same place because of the lack of support and all my different challenges, but I have to keep fighting for a better life for me and my son. I don't want Shaka to ever experience the same struggle I have been going through.

Sometimes I wonder if he might someday write his own book about our struggle. The one good thing I have noticed is that he always relives the good memories. I hope he doesn't remember the bad ones. I will continue to work as hard as I can to support him in everything he wants to do. With the lack of both physical and financial support from his father, it hasn't been the easiest of times, but I do my best to stay strong and focused for him.

As far as relationships go, there's definitely light at the end of the tunnel. Towards the end of 2017, I met someone I truly believe is the love of my life. We met in such an unconventional way, but we just clicked right from the beginning.

After the bad relationship I had with my ex, I was scared to start any new relationship or even trust anyone in my life. I didn't know if I'd ever find someone who would love me as much as I love them. I was tired of being single, therefore I decided to get back to the dating world.

The first guy I dated seemed nice in the beginning, but we were opposites. We disagreed on pretty much everything we did, and it just wasn't working for both of us. I dealt with it for a while because I was

a little bit desperate to find someone new in my life and my son's life. I was excited when I found out he was a father because he would be able to understand how to support my son.

However, that relationship was very rocky. In fact, one time he called me and said he was thinking about getting back with his ex, and we broke up. I stayed single for a couple of months and enjoyed my life.

One day I was out with my friend and received a text from him saying he missed me. The text caught me off guard because I wasn't sure if he really missed me or if he just missed me because he had seen my new photos on one of the social media platforms. I decided to talk to him and get a better understanding of what he meant.

We decided to give the relationship a new trial and see where it would go. The relationship was still very rocky because we had different expectations of each other. We also lived in different states—he was in California, and I lived in Minnesota. –

In October, for his birthday, I decided to take a trip and surprise him for his birthday. I booked my flight, hotel, and planned it around his work schedule.

For some reason, my instinct kept telling me it might be a bad idea to surprise him. I was hinting at seeing him every time he and I talked, but he didn't sound like he would be happy if I surprised him. Because of that, I decided to tell him about the trip. He wasn't happy with the whole idea and thought it wasn't a good time.

From that day on, the relationship was not the same. We weren't in tune as we were before. Our relationship reminded me of the one I had with Peter. I was so tired of the fighting. I wanted to have a relationship with no fights, especially around Shaka. I wanted him to have a normal, loving family with both adults living amicably and happy. I prayed every night for God to show me the way and guide me.

As they say, God never fails us, and no situation is too big for him.

While I was still trying to figure out my relationship, I started to date one person online. When I started talking to this new person, it was a complete surprise because he was so different from the person I was dating. I knew I was a hopeless romantic. But because I'd been catfished previously, I was nervous. The guy told me everything I wanted to hear, which had me scared and confused at first. Thankfully, things became clearer over time.

And part of how this relationship came about was kind of unconventional because I swore I would never do any online or long-distance dating again. I was scammed by some guy who pretended to be one of the celebrities I had a long-time crush on. Of course, it was too good to be true. I thought it only happened to people who are careless, but there I was getting scammed by a little teenager in Nigeria.

A friend and I later found out who he was, and he admitted everything he had done. I was so embarrassed that I not only went through that experience, but it was a small little boy behind it. He got money and a whole brand-new phone from me. I couldn't believe how I fell for him so quickly when I had never met him in my life. Because of that, I decided to never participate in any form of online dating.

In fact, I ended up marrying him. Sometimes you never know where you're going to meet the most beautiful people in life. Our relationship is proof that because something didn't work out the first time, it doesn't mean you should give up on it.

CHAPTER 11

WHERE I'M GOING

Fast forward to a few months down the road, when I broke off the relationship I was in and decided to focus on the new guy I started dating online even though he lived in Ghana. I was still in Minneapolis. Both of my former long-distance relationships didn't work for me at all. So, when I say trying this new relationship was a long shot, it was really one.

We talked for a few months online, over the phone. He seemed too good to be true because he said all the things I wanted to hear from a man. Of course, it was scary, and we had to build trust over time.

I literally spent hours on the phone with him—every extra minute I had. Sometimes we even stayed on the phone the whole night without knowing. Our connection grew stronger each time we talked, but it's one thing to talk over the phone versus seeing someone in person.

I finally decided to go visit him for the first time in Ghana. It would be my first trip back to Africa in over sixteen years. I was scared just like anyone would be, not knowing what to expect. But I wanted to give the relationship my best effort.

We were both excited about the visit. I was a hopeless romantic, but

I never believed in fairy tales. I never understood what people meant when they said that you know you've met the love of your life when you meet them for the first time and your heart skips, and you feel butterflies in your stomach.

I felt all those things the first time I laid my eyes on him. I was so happy to see and hug him. After we left the airport, we went and got roasted fish. Neither one of us could stop smiling.

He took care of me the whole time I was in Ghana. Anything I wanted or needed, he got it for me. It didn't matter how much it cost or where it was, he always said yes. This was somewhat of a new treatment for me because I was so used to doing things for all the men in my life besides the time when I was with Jay. I fully enjoyed my stay with him, meeting his friends and family. Everything went as I imagined it and much more.

I came home from that trip thinking that I had finally found the man for me. A man who understood me and would treat me the way I always wanted to be treated. I was excited to introduce him to my family. I knew it wasn't going to be easy because my family is very critical of every person I introduce to them. I was ready to finally settle down though—nothing fazed me. I didn't care what anyone was going to think about him being from a different country than I was. In my culture, people would rather you marry someone from the same culture. However, I had long ago vowed to never date or even marry someone from my own culture. Even though I was very excited that my new man wasn't anywhere close to my culture, the struggle would be introducing him to my family and them accepting him.

He and I took a few more months talking over the phone before we both agreed it was time for him to meet my family. At that point, he was ready to make a commitment to me, too. He was ready to fully embrace my family and ask them if he could marry me.

I was so excited for that next big step although I didn't know how my family was going to react to that news. I told my family about him first because I was so excited to do things a little bit differently than last time. They were excited to meet him and see what he had to offer.

We set up a date for him to go visit my family and marry me traditionally. It was a small wedding in Freetown with just a few family members.

I was happy that he took that big step to marry me traditionally. In my culture that is actually the wedding that matters. Once we got married, we were official and could start a family of our own. We started the process to bring him to the U.S. so we could start a family here. Eventually we want to settle in Ghana, but first we wanted to live in the U.S. because of all the different opportunities available.

While we were waiting for his visa, I made a couple of more trips to Ghana to spend quality time with him. We decided to try to get pregnant so that when he was finally able to move here, we would already have a child on the way. It took a couple of trips before that happened.

On my last trip to visit him before he could join me in America, I decided to take my son with me so the two of them could bond. They got along so well, which made me extremely happy. He was a great father to my son and took great care of him throughout the whole time we were in Ghana.

On that same trip, I found out I was pregnant. That whole trip was a dream come true because everything I hoped for happened. I was happy to know that I was about to start a whole new family with a man that would be by my side as I had always wanted. I was happy for that next chapter in my life, though it would be a while before he could join me and Saka in Minnesota.

Shaka and I left Ghana and went home to wait for to come to us.

Although the pregnancy was good news, it was very painful from the beginning. I was in the hospital every other day from the time we came back from Ghana. I was in so much pain. I was sad all the time, and my husband was sad too because he couldn't be there to help me through the difficult days and nights.

I was fortunate and grateful that I had a job that was very understanding. I couldn't work. I was sick and miserable the whole time, but I kept telling myself that it would get better as the pregnancy progressed. Everyone kept telling me the pregnancy would get easier as time went on.

When I was pregnant with Shaka, it was the easiest pregnancy compared to most pregnancies. I had some issues and was in and out of the hospital due to my anxiety, but overall it was an easy pregnancy. I didn't even know I was pregnant for about four months because I never got sick. I thought the other pregnancy would be the same way. I was hoping it would be smoother overall because I had all the support I needed and didn't have from my first pregnancy. In addition, this was a planned pregnancy. Since I was married, and I had already introduced my husband to my family, I was excited to tell them about it.

I told my mother about this pregnancy because I knew she was going to be happy for me this time since we did everything the proper way by first getting married before I got pregnant. She was happy for me when I told her, just like everyone else. Despite the love, support, and happiness, I just kept getting sicker every day.

One afternoon I was in so much pain I had to go to the emergency room. I didn't know where the pain came from nor do I ever want to experience it again. It was the worst pain I have ever experienced in my life (even worse than when I had my son). When we got to the ER, they ran all types of tests and later discovered that I had fibroids in my womb. I always knew I had them; in fact, when I went for my first exam

when I got pregnant, the OBGYN said the fibroids would not affect the pregnancy at all. I was happy to hear that because I didn't know what to expect. She told me how big they were, but she said they wouldn't be an issue at all.

When we got the ER, I told the doctor about the fibroids. He ran more tests and later confirmed that one of the fibroids had grown bigger. He gave me some pain medication that was considered safe for pregnant women.

I went home that same night feeling a lot better. However, the following day when the medication started wearing off, the pain came back. It was much worse than what I experienced the day before. I took more prescription painkillers; I put a hot towel on my stomach. I moved around the apartment because they said moving helps you feel better. Nothing helped.

I was miserable but didn't want to go back to the ER right away because I knew they weren't going to do anything different than what they'd already done. But eventually, the pain got so bad that I had to go back to the ER.

On my way to the hospital, I my water broke, which shouldn't have happened because I was just four months pregnant. I didn't want to think the worst, but in my mind, I already had that bad feeling that something bad had happened.

By the time I got to the hospital I was bleeding heavily, but I still had a little bit of hope that it could be something else. I was given a room right away and they started running some tests to see if the baby was still okay. A few hours later the doctor broke the news no woman ever wants to hear he told me that I had lost the baby.

I didn't want to believe it right away because I was only concerned about the pain I was experiencing at the time. I was heartbroken to hear the news but decided to focus on trying to get the pain level down.

Eventually when the pain was in control, it finally hit me that I had lost the baby.

I began crying endlessly because I was so ready to be a mother again. I called my husband to let him know what had happened. I felt terrible because his mother had been asking for a grandchild since he and I met. I thought I was finally going to make that dream happen for her. I was so heartbroken to know that wasn't going to be the case right away. Not only was I crying because I lost my child, but I was also feeling bad for my husband and that he had to break the news to his family.

Losing the baby was one of the hardest things I've had to experience. It's hard to talk about without crying because it hurts to this day. The worst part of it all is that I couldn't be with my husband so we could console each other. I had to stay in the hospital for another week or so because I was still in so much pain.

Everyone kept saying that maybe since I was in so much pain when I was pregnant, I would now feel a little bit better. I didn't because every day I just kept getting sick and the pain was still very bad. I was later told it was because the fibroids were dying off. When the fibroids lose blood, they eventually die. I was happy they were doing so, but I was still in so much pain and getting more frustrated every day.

People recommended different things to me to help with the pain. The doctors prescribed all the strongest painkillers, but they barely helped. My ex mother-in-law eventually recommended a product called "black seed," which is both a seed and an oil.

I took it, and that helped me gradually get better and helped me begin feeling like myself again. I was grateful for that, but I was still very sad and fragile because I lost the one thing I was looking forward to the most.

To this day I still don't understand what happened, and still feel sad. I tried looking for answers, but my doctor said it was hard to pinpoint

one thing that could have caused the issue. She said we will never know, but even she was surprised because it isn't common to lose a baby at four months. She said fibroids could have been an issue, but she didn't want to say that was the main cause of it all. I later started making peace with it because I know everything happens for a reason.

After the miscarriage, my husband began the process of moving here permanently. I started looking forward to the future, as it helped take my mind off the miscarriage. I am so grateful that at the time it happened, I had a lot of support from both people around me and those who lived far away. My husband's family checked on me as much as they could. My husband checked on me to make sure I didn't think I was going through this on my own. Even my sister came to live with me for a couple of weeks to make sure I felt loved and supported.

The one person who was with me through it all was Morgan who was with me every step of the way. It would have been impossible to go through that difficult time without her.

She was with me from the first day Shaka and I got back from Ghana, when I wasn't feeling well. She took good care of me by providing everything I asked for. Sometimes I would ask for the impossible, but she never gave up nor got mad at me.

I remember when I asked her to make me tea a certain way. Every time she brought it and it didn't taste the way I wanted it to, I yelled at her to make it again. Not once did she complain about anything.

Some days I was so emotional and would just be mad at her even though she was helping me. She would be upset for a second, and I felt bad, but she didn't hold anything against me. She spent sleepless nights lying on the floor with me. Anything I wanted to do; she was right there to help me through it all. I remember one time when we had just become friends, when she said she hated people that spit or seeing vomit. However, when I was pregnant she handled everything. I was

spitting a lot every time and everywhere. Sometimes I would lie next to her and just start spitting in a cup she'd gotten me. I could tell she was uncomfortable, but not once did she complain about it at all.

Every time I needed to vomit and needed someone to rub my back, I would call her even when she was sleeping. She was there right away. The countless times we went to the emergency room, she stayed with me while I waited for hours for a bed. Every time I freaked out because I was in so much pain, she calmed me down and said everything was going to be okay.

When I was in the hospital, people would visit for short amounts of time, but she would sleep right there with me in the tiny, cold bed. She only left me for a few hours to go shower, and then she'd go right back to the hospital. My emotions were all over the place, but she handled it very well.

The day of the miscarriage we almost didn't sleep for twelve plus hours. At least I got a chance to sleep, but she was sitting right there with me from the time we go to the hospital to the time we left. I couldn't believe how much she did for me. She stayed calm through the hardest part of my life. She calmed me down to make sure I didn't lose my mind. The day my water broke, and I knew I had lost the baby, I told her I knew it and started freaking out. She told me to stay calm until the hospital confirms it. I already knew what had happened, but she managed to keep me calm and strong throughout the whole process. She filled the gap and support I needed when my husband wasn't there. She continues to support me every day without hesitation. Sometimes we meet people in our lives that become more than family. I still tell her every day that God sent her to me to be my guardian angel because she has been that and much more.

Although that pregnancy didn't end as I envisioned it, I am grateful to know that I have so much support in my life now. I know by God's

grace I will have more kids with my husband. I am especially happy to know that I have so many supportive people around me to help with another pregnancy. Maybe it wasn't time for me to have that child then. Sometimes it is hard to know the plans God has for us, but it is important to stay patient and believe that something good will always come out of the struggles we go through. That story is part of me now and a reminder to me that things won't always go as I plan them. God always has his own plans for us, and we just have to trust and believe that everything will always work out in the end. I've learned a lot from that experience and hope to become a better person because of it.

CHAPTER 12

CONCLUSION

I am still finding my way, but it looks like I can close the door on a lot of my previous struggles. I am about to start a beautiful new family with an amazing husband and son. I look forward to having more children. It looks like God is starting to answer all my prayers by giving me everything I've been asking for and much more.

I could have given up because I felt like the whole world was against me. But I'm so glad I didn't because all my dreams are coming together. I still plan on opening my restaurant at some point. I eventually want to move back to Ghana and settle there with my children and husband. Our goal is to work hard and save as much as possible so that we can accomplish that goal. Once we do, I want to open a restaurant there. Most of the restaurants in Ghana only service Ghanaian food, and my dream is to create one that serves a variety of foods from all over the world. It's a big goal, and I will make it work by any means necessary.

It is always hard to predict what the future holds, but at this point, it looks bright for me because of all the plans and support I have. Sometimes going through struggle leads you to good things.

Most people thought I would never make it because I had a child

at such a young age and had to sacrifice a lot. Honestly, I believe that was the best thing to ever happen to me because I learned a lot from my struggles and pains.

My son is now growing and starting to become more responsible. I am very optimistic that when me and my husband add to our family, he will be a great big brother. He knows how to take care of himself. He has a few challenges just like all kids at his age, and he experienced a lot of trauma from the time Peter and I were together. But now that we have a new family and a good support system, he is starting to come around and be his happy self again.

Now that I have dealt with those struggles, I'm ready for all the good things and will not take anything for granted. I am excited for this new future and what it holds for me. It might be too late for me to become a model because that is what most people will say. However, I still believe in my potential.

I recently started an Instagram page(matuadventures) that focuses on my selling other people's products. I also started my own YouTube channel (Matu Adventures) that focuses on family, my adventures, and inspirational content. If I don't ever live the dream of being a model, I still want to be involved in entertainment however I can. I'm a people person.

I have learned a lot of things and want to give some advice of my own that I could have used along the way. No matter how old you are, from the time you discover something isn't right, always try to speak up even if you're scared. Don't be scared of people not believing you because when you wait too long people might not believe you at that point. Always tell someone when something bad happens without worrying about the fear of any repercussions or punishments. There are always people who will believe you.

We African women tend to hold things inside because we don't want

to shame our family, but it is the wrong thing to do. African women are taught to put themselves last before anyone else, but we have to speak up first and do what is right. Life will always leave you behind if you don't put yourself first. Men will always leave you and find someone else if you think you're doing them a favor by putting them first. If you put yourself first and don't put up with disrespect, it means you're powerful and independent. If you fall, get up and try again. There's no place it says you can't try again. You can always try until you feel like you have accomplished what you want. Even if people give up on you and doubt you, never give up until you get what you want.

Friends are sometimes better than family. Always find that one person who will be there for you and lead you in the right direction. Have that one friend to lean on who will be loyal to you and stay with you and listen to you every time you need a shoulder to cry on.

Mothers, especially single mothers, be patient and be a mother to your child. It doesn't matter if the father is present, just be there for your child. Don't do things for your kids expecting something in return. Your child is a gift; therefore, it is a gift you're responsible for. The child didn't choose to be born; you gave birth to them. Always treat them like the biggest treasure because they are a gift from God that not every woman gets to experience. Provide for the children without thinking about the rewards you will get from taking care of them. If they grow up and choose to pay you back, let it be their personal choice and not because they owe you something.

THE END